# THE HAPPY DOG COOKBOOK

# THE HAPPY DOG COOKBOOK

Sean McCormack
featuring Annabel Karmel

# Contents

# Foreword

—

*From Annabel Karmel*

'Everyone thinks they have the best dog.
 And none of them are wrong.'

– W. R. Purche

There are two things you need to know about me. One: I have three dogs and if I were to live in a dogs-only world, I'd be pretty fluent in dog speak. I understand every bark, yap and howl, just as I would tune in to my children's cries and coos when they were tiny.

Two: I love food. In fact, I live for food. I've authored 46 cookbooks to help families explore a world of good food. Yet my dogs unquestionably pip me to the post in the food-loving stakes. There is an outside chance my American cocker spaniel Bono would sell me out for a piece of roast chicken.

We consider our canines to be fully paid-up members of the family. They quickly earn their stripes, and in two shakes of a dog's tail you're succumbing to those puppy dog eyes and sharing your Sunday roast (let alone your sofa, your bed and slobbery kisses). But it's not all in vain; did you know that the 'feel-good' hormone oxytocin peaks in both people and dogs when they interact positively? That's right, research shows that dogs really do love us back!

I think it's safe to say that the doggy feel-good factor runs high in my home – both among humans and hounds. My brood, Bono, Hamilton and Sabre definitely rule the roost, and I always say that my partner comes fifth place in my house hierarchy, after my three dogs and a vacancy for another dog!

My days spent in the kitchen recipe testing and batch cooking wouldn't be complete without my drooling trio tracing my every move, waiting for the smallest of scraps. So I'm no stranger to adapting my failsafe family favourites for my four-legged kitchen helpers to chow down on. After all, why shouldn't they enjoy treats made with the same quality and care as our own food?

Having raised dogs all my life, I know that their nutritional needs are very different to ours. Their digestive system is uniquely canine and should be managed sensitively, no matter how much they beg to chomp on your cheese toastie or bark for that spare rasher of bacon. And because doggy diets differ depending on breed, age, size and lifestyle, knowing what to feed them can be a bit of a mutt minefield, especially if you do want to offer them homemade treats.

Two legs or four, we should all be fulfilled by good, wholesome food, and that's why I'm honoured to be a part of this incredible recipe book for dogs. These delicious treat ideas, expertly developed by vet and canine nutritional expert Sean McCormack, are packed with tail-wagging goodness. And you don't need to be a seasoned chef to make these recipes. Each treat has been designed with simplicity in mind. And you'll be the best cook in your dog's eyes in any case!

And because life is better when we cook together, I wanted to bring my decades of family food expertise to the table with my own tried and tested dog recipes that even the youngest family members can help prepare for your pooch.

Beautifully photographed, with easy-to-follow nutritional guidance, this cookbook is one you'll want to use time and time again – your dog won't have it any other way!

# Introduction

Our dogs are members of the family, and nourishing them with healthy and delicious treats is a powerful bond builder. Who doesn't love the waggling-tailed dance our dogs do when it's feeding time? I know I do!

I've grown up with dogs. My first dog, a little white terrier called Sheba, is in my opinion the greatest dog that ever lived. She was my best buddy, and I have fond memories of preparing special meals for her. Each Sunday, I would ask for leftovers from our roast to give her because I wanted her to enjoy a special treat too. If we had a slap-up lunch, why couldn't Sheba? This was especially true on Christmas day; preparing Sheba her festive feast was always a highlight for me – and, of course, for her!

The recipes I have chosen to include here are inspired by many happy years spent with dogs – from Sheba to the dogs I have been lucky to be surrounded by my entire professional life. I've learnt that the process of coming to understand your canine companion, getting to know what foods they love, developing recipes for them and treating them is an important and joyful part of the dog–owner relationship. I want to help you create delicious, sometimes indulgent, but always nutritious, home-cooked treats for your dog that can be given without guilt.

Before the recipes, I want to start with the nutrition basics, giving you the tools and understanding to make sensible decisions around your dog's diet, weight and overall health that will ensure a long, healthy and happy life. There are three simple rules:

> Creating your own treats means you know exactly what you are feeding your pet

### Tailor your dog's diet

No two dogs are the same, so tailoring a dog's diet to their specific needs can make a world of difference to their health, happiness and comfort. For example, my canine sidekick at work, Border terrier Monty, has a very sensitive stomach. If he eats most commercial treats he can really drop a few stinkers in the office. Not pleasant. Instead, treating him with fresh simple ingredients and going grain free has really helped his digestive issues. His absolute favourite treats are the Guilt-Free Breakfast Bakes (see page 66).

### Choose the right ingredients

The ingredients that I have put into the treats are also significant. Creating your own treats means you know exactly what you are feeding your pet – from healthy fresh vegetables and lean meat, to those 'superfood' ingredients that will help you to ease their aching joints and give them glossy coats and happy smiles in no time.

### Feed your dog the right amount

Finally, it would be unwise to ignore the issue of rising pet obesity when writing a book about treat recipes for dogs. Making sensible decisions around your dog's diet, weight and overall health, and in particular making sure you feed your dog the right amount, will ensure a long, healthy and happy life.

Over the years I've talked to thousands of concerned owners about their dogs' health issues and, in particular, diet and weight management. Being overweight or obese makes life just that little bit harder for your pet, even though they often don't show it. Excess weight slows them down when they'd love to play; it makes stiff, old joints just a bit more uncomfortable; it makes exercise a struggle;

and it makes getting on the sofa, into the car or going upstairs to bed more tricky. Overweight pets tend to enjoy life a little less.

The best feeling in the world for me as a vet is when I help a dog shift the excess weight that's crept up on them over the years. The overwhelming response from their owner is: 'I just can't believe the difference it's made. She's like a puppy again!' It genuinely fills me with delight.

As well as Monty and the rest of the team at tails.com, I'm delighted to be working alongside Annabel Karmel, proud owner of three dogs and celebrated author on feeding young families. I'm hoping that by combining my knowledge of dog health and nutrition alongside Annabel's expertise as family feeding expert will help you make great choices when treating your dog. Annabel has kindly contributed some beautiful, tasty and nutritious recipes for the book, which I'm sure you'll enjoy making and your dog will enjoy tasting.

If we're going to treat the pups in our life, it's absolutely possible to maximise the benefit. Given in moderation as part of a balanced feeding plan, healthy, delicious, enjoyable treats can introduce a wider range of foods to a dog's diet, can be used as incentives for training, and – perhaps most importantly – can cement that wonderful bond between you and your dog. It's a win-win for happy dogs and owners. Let me show you how.

– *Sean*

Healthy, delicious, enjoyable treats can cement that wonderful bond between you and your dog

# Nutrition *for* dogs

# Tailor Your Dog's Diet

No two
dogs are
the same

No two dogs are the same. Within the same breed needs differ, and even siblings from the same litter often end up having different dietary needs.

So what matters when it comes to a dog's individual needs? Well, there are few key factors that impact what a dog needs and when.

## Breed

Different breeds of dog are more likely to suffer from specific dietary issues. Dalmatians, for example, can be prone to urinary stones if not fed the right diet, while northern breeds like huskies and malamutes are more likely to have a zinc deficiency. There are more general breed effects, too; working breeds, such as collies, shepherds and springer spaniels, need more energy to sustain their increased activity levels. And of course, larger breeds of dogs will have very different caloric requirements to smaller ones, and will also need different nutrients at different stages of their development.

## Age and life stage

The nutrients a puppy needs are different to those that an adult or senior dog may need. They may have higher calorie needs to support their growth, and a greater proportion of this caloric requirement might come from protein, which is important for development. Protein is best given in easily digestible forms, such as chicken or fish, as puppies can often have sensitive tummies.

At this young age, a dog's immune system is strengthening, so it's very important that we provide them with a diet rich in antioxidants from vegetables. As they develop, puppies also benefit from a carefully balanced calcium and phosphorus intake over time to strengthen quickly growing bones. In fact, making sure young dogs are supported can even help to pre-empt bone troubles later in life.

Do also be aware that large and small breeds mature at different rates. For example, a chihuahua puppy needs a different diet to what a giant breed, such as a Great Dane, needs as a puppy. There a lot of variables that you could get quite geeky about, so if this is something you would like to explore further, I recommend discussing it in more detail with your vet.

I often hear dog owners say: 'Oh, he put all that weight on when he got neutered.' In most cases, neutering happens at the very time a dog is becoming an adult and their weight is stabilising. If we don't control their calorie allowance from this point in time, their weight will begin to climb. We all know how much food human teenagers can put away and not gain weight, and dogs are similar. We just have to remember that when they reach adulthood, they will have a slightly slower metabolism and we need to ensure that we match the amount of food we give them to how much activity and exercise their lifestyle entails.

Older dogs may benefit from more joint-supportive ingredients, such as those with anti-inflammatory action like salmon oil. As many breeds lose muscle condition and can become thin in old age, extra good fats are also helpful for maintaining body condition.

Large and small breeds mature at different rates

**DID YOU KNOW?**

Smaller dog breeds grow quicker than larger ones – while chihuahuas finish growing as early as 9–10 months, Great Danes can take in excess of 24 months. Smaller breeds also tend to live longer.

Food really
is the first
medicine

## Weight

If your dog is overweight, you'll need to reduce the amount of food given, including my delicious treats, I'm afraid. It would also be wise to increase the amount of exercise your dog is getting – but don't think of it as a chore. Dogs love spending time with us and they'll feel far more grateful for getting out and about than we would if someone forced us onto the treadmill! It keeps us fit too, so it's win-win.

If your dog is underweight, boosting their calories with more nutrient-dense foods or a larger amount of food is a good idea. We'll discuss weight issues more in Feed Your Dog the Right Amount (page 39).

## Health conditions

The really magic thing about nutrition for me as a vet is that I can help many pets just by making recommendations on their diet – food really is the first medicine. For example, did you know that skin and digestive issues are the top two reasons for dogs being brought to the vet? Both of these can be influenced with diet, and many of the treats in this book are packed with beneficial ingredients to support dogs with issues, from itchy skin (see Cranberry & Linseed Valentine Hearts, page 58) to sensitive digestion (see Orchard Fruit Flapjacks, page 86), to stiff joints (see Sean's Savoury Superfood Muffins, page 80).

If your dog has itchy, dry skin, they can benefit from a diet rich in essential fatty acids, such as omega-3 and omega-6, which help support the skin and boost its immune function.

A glossy, healthy coat is often a welcome result of a diet rich in essential fatty acids, too. If your dog has a food allergy, this can also result in dry, itchy and flaky skin.

Digestive issues can be really frustrating to get to the bottom of (pardon the pun), for vets and owners alike – not to mention how uncomfortable they are for our poor pups. You can support your dog's digestive health by adjusting fibre levels or adding beneficial ingredients like prebiotics, beetroot or certain seeds. But if their condition is down to a dietary intolerance, excluding the offending ingredients is the main way to manage these.

## Allergies and intolerances

Because we tend to feed our dogs such a wide range of foods, treats, chews, scraps and titbits, it can be really hard to pin down exactly what our dog might be allergic or intolerant to. It also doesn't help that many of the symptoms of food allergy overlap with those of environmental allergies.

Start by simplifying the list of ingredients you're feeding (don't forget treats) and excluding the suspected culprits. Your vet is a great source of help if you're really struggling to work out if food is the issue for dogs with skin and digestive problems. And some pet food companies have excellent customer service lines with trained canine nutrition teams for that very reason. One of the reasons I'm so passionate about the work we do at tails.com is that we can help individual customers with specific problems.

When choosing what to feed your dog, keep in mind their specific health concerns and it will likely benefit their well-being.

# Temperament

It's also worth quickly mentioning temperament here. Although the link between this and diet are less concrete than the physiological benefits of particular foods, there is some evidence to suggest that if your dog is particularly fearful or anxious, introducing certain foods to their diet may help.

Some of the ingredients that can help with anxiety are turkey, chamomile and pumpkin (see Choose the Right Ingredients, pages 26–37, for more on these). I've included these ingredients in my seasonal treat

Some ingredients can help fearful dogs with anxiety

recipes like Calming Halloween Pumpkin Chews (see page 95) and my Christmassy Turkey, Broccoli & Cranberry Bites (see page 109) when things can get a little tense for the more fearful pups in the household.

I always say to dog owners to have realistic expectations though. If your dog is climbing the walls in terror during fireworks season, then diet and supplements will only be a calming aid; they're not likely to be a magic cure. Some behavioural training and treatment is also needed alongside, and in the lead up to the anxious period.

## SUMMARY:

– No two dogs are the same; every single dog will have unique nutritional requirements.

– Supporting your dog nutritionally at each stage of their life can help to prevent problems developing later in life.

– If your dog is overweight, feed less and exercise more.

– Certain foods can help to ease health conditions, such as issues with digestion or skin complaints.

– Food allergies and intolerances should be identified, and the culprit foods excluded from your dog's diet.

– Including certain ingredients in the diets of anxious dogs may help to calm them.

# Choose the Right Ingredients

I've chosen all the ingredients in these recipes to provide a benefit.

Whether that's because they are super tasty, provide support for certain health complaints, or just keep our dogs in glorious condition, you won't find any nasties here.

I've divided the various ingredients used in the recipes into proteins and fats, carbohydrates, fruit and vegetables, and supplements. I'm going to openly admit here that I'm a bit of a nutrition geek – it's fascinating. I hope by explaining what everything does, you find it interesting and useful too.

## Proteins & Fats

Proteins provide a range of amino acids, which are important building blocks for your dog to grow, as well as maintain and repair their body. Protein comes from both plant and animal sources, and each ingredient will provide a different complement of amino acids. Dogs need ten essential amino acids in order to thrive. Choose a complete and balanced main food for your dog and they will be covered for all ten, but my treats can help provide nutritional extras.

Healthy fats in moderation are vital for lots of body functions, including supporting joint health and boosting skin condition, leading to lovely glossy coats. But not all fats are created equal. Omega-3 fat from salmon, for example, is far healthier than saturated animal fat from bacon rind. And as all fats are rich sources of energy, they can lead to weight gain if dogs are given too much. Be careful not to overdo it, particularly when it comes to treats.

**ALMONDS:** a small amount of ground almonds in baked treats adds a flavour that dogs enjoy, along with a little protein. But go easy – almonds are high in fat. Whole nuts in general are not recommended for dogs, as they can be a choking hazard.

**BACON:** is here purely for its appetising flavour and aroma, which dogs and humans alike find oh so appealing. Bacon is quite calorific, so bear in mind that a little goes a very long way mixed into a recipe. The fat is best trimmed off if preparing it for your dog. My high-reward Bacon & Apple Crunchies (page 91) harness the drool appeal of bacon, so you can teach your dog backflips if you want to! Bacon treats (and backflips) are best avoided in old dogs or those with kidney issues, due to bacon's high salt content.

**BEEF:** a great source of healthy protein, rich in essential amino acids, vitamins and minerals, and with a flavour most dogs relish, beef is a fantastic ingredient. Choose lean cuts and lean beef mince as too much fat can upset digestion, as well as being high in calories.

**CHEESE:** a good source of protein and calcium but can be fattening in large amounts, so use sparingly. Most dogs are lactose intolerant, so although they often love the flavour of cheese, it's always best to use a lactose-free version.

**CHICKEN:** is a highly digestible, lean protein source with a great range of amino acids, as well as omega-6 for healthy skin and glucosamine for supporting joint health.

**EGGS:** are a great source of protein; they are considered to have the perfect amino acid profile for dogs, as all the essential amino acids are present in balance.

**HAM:** similar to bacon but generally lower in fat, ham is OK to use as an occasional treat. Dogs will really work for it, so harness its appeal for training and games that will challenge your dog to learn new skills. Make sure it's not overly processed or salted ham you use – pick one with no artificial flavours, colourings or preservatives.

**HEART:** organ meat is a highly nutritious source of lean protein, vitamins and important minerals like iron – and dogs love the flavour. You can source beef or lamb heart from your local butcher, or sometimes the meat counter in your local supermarket. I know it's not appealing to some, but I'm a big believer that if we eat meat, we should always use the whole animal, whether that's for our own consumption or for our pets.

## DID YOU KNOW?

Glucosamine can play a part in keeping ligaments, tendons, cartilage and joint fluid working well. It provides the building blocks for the body to produce glycosaminoglycans (GAGs), which are extremely important for maintaining healthy joints.

**KIDNEY:** a highly nutritious organ meat you can source from your butcher or on the meat counter of the supermarket. It's a taste dogs love – try it out and see for yourself.

**LAMB:** a tasty and nutritious source of protein, lamb is also hypoallergenic for many dogs; if your dog has adverse reactions to many foods, lamb could help things settle. Additionally, grass-fed lamb contains conjugated linoleic acid, which can actually help promote fat metabolism. But let's get real, lamb isn't a magical fat buster. Just like anything, if you feed your dog just a bit too much, it will lead to weight gain.

**LIVER:** is a great occasional, nutritious and tasty treat. It's nutrient rich, with high levels of amino acids, fats and vitamins A and B, as well as minerals like copper, iron and zinc.

**MILK:** is a source of protein and most dogs enjoy the taste, but it is included in the recipes primarily as a useful baking ingredient. Most dogs are lactose intolerant, so dairy products are generally a no-go unless they're lactose free.

**PEANUTS AND PEANUT BUTTER:** are a rich source of fats and proteins, but they're not particularly well balanced so shouldn't be a dietary staple. It's no secret that dogs go wild for the taste and texture of peanut butter. It's perfect as an occupier treat, smeared in a Kong feeder or on a lick mat, but it is quite calorific, so use sparingly. And finally, always make sure the peanut butter you feed your dog is free of the sweetener xylitol, which is toxic to dogs.

## DID YOU KNOW?

Puppies get DHA from their mother's milk. When DHA is supplemented after puppies have been weaned, the puppies have been shown to have improved learning abilities and socialisation outcomes, and it also aids their vision development over time.

**SALMON:** really is a superfood, with many health benefits for dogs of all ages and nutritional needs. It's especially beneficial for dogs with sensitive tummies as it's highly digestible. Salmon is super for our golden oldies with stiff joints, or pain from arthritis, as it is rich in omega-3 fatty acids, clinically proven to fight inflammation. It's also great for young growing dogs, with the omega-3 fatty acid docosahexaenoic acid (DHA) helping their mental and vision development. It's a good source of B12, choline, potassium and selenium, as well as containing strong antioxidants. Let's all give it up for salmon!

**TURKEY:** a wonderful, lean, healthy and highly digestible protein source, with the added benefit of being rich in the amino acid tryptophan. Dogs (and humans) use this amino acid to produce the feel-good, calming hormone serotonin, so a turkey treat at times when dogs are anxious could be helpful.

**YOGHURT:** is a good source of calcium and probiotics. Make sure it's a lactose-free version for dogs, as most are intolerant to this sugar found in dairy products.

# Carbohydrates

Carbohydrates are a great source of energy for day-to-day activities and fuelling all that ball chasing, jumping, and rough and tumble play our dogs love. They're an important part of a dog's diet, and should be given in balance with quality protein.

Despite some claims otherwise, dogs are not exclusive carnivores but true omnivores, evolved to thrive by feeding on animal and plant ingredients. Cereals and whole grains are an excellent source of slow-release carbohydrate energy, fibre and B vitamins, as well as many important minerals. Some dogs do better on a grain-free diet for various reasons, including food allergies and intolerances. But most grain-free diets are not carbohydrate free; they may include other nutritious, delicious sources of carbohydrate energy which your dog needs, such as potatoes.

**OATS AND OATMEAL:** a highly nutritious, easily digested source of slow-release carbohydrate energy. They are rich in fibre, B vitamins, zinc, iron, manganese, phosphorus and selenium.

**POTATOES:** a very easily digestible source of carbohydrate and an excellent source of vitamins C and B6, as well as potassium, which is good for immunity and energy production. They are also a source of non-meat protein and complement the amino acids present in meat and fish proteins.

**RICE AND RICE FLOUR:** a highly digestible carbohydrate and protein source that is gentle on the stomach. It provides a wide range of nutrients including B vitamins and iron. Choose brown rice if you can, as it contains more fibre.

**WHEAT:** is highly nutritious in its wholegrain form. It's an excellent source of energy-giving carbohydrate, as well as fibre, B vitamins and the mineral manganese. But wheat is a much-misunderstood ingredient; a protein in wheat, called gluten, is problematic for some people to digest. However, unlike in humans, coeliac disease or true gluten allergy is very rare in dogs. If your dog is reactive to foods containing wheat, I've included some gluten-free alternatives which can be substituted in recipes such as my Pup-Friendly Hot Cross Buns (page 61).

# Fruit & Vegetables

Fruit and vegetables are an important part of your dog's diet, packing a serious punch of health-giving vitamins and minerals, as well as fibre, which is important for digestive health. Many of them are rich sources of antioxidants – a range of natural compounds including certain vitamins and plant extracts, such as carotenoids and polyphenols – which help protect the body against cell damage and strengthen immune defences. Giving healthy vegetable-based treats to dogs with weight issues instead of those packed with more calorific ingredients is a great way to treat them without adding too many excess calories. Raw carrots and green beans are a firm favourite with most of the dogs in my life.

**APPLE:** provides dietary fibre, vitamins A and C, and antioxidants, in particular polyphenols. These plant compounds have a protective function for cells, and have even been shown to improve dental hygiene, by reducing the accumulation of plaque and tartar that leads to gum disease. Obviously too much fruit sugar isn't the best idea for dental health though, so vegetable sources of polyphenols are preferred.

**BANANA:** most dogs I know just love bananas. They are famously rich in potassium, which supports the nervous and muscular systems. Bananas can be high in sugar and calories, so a little not a lot is the order of the day.

**BEETROOT:** very good for us and for our pups! Beetroot is rich in vitamin C, folate, potassium and manganese, as well as the fibre required for healthy digestion.

**BLACKBERRIES:** are a good source of vitamin C, dietary fibre and potassium. They are also a rich source of antioxidants, in particular plant polyphenols – the powerhouse of the antioxidant world!

**BLUEBERRIES:** are absolutely bursting with cell-protecting antioxidants to boost immune function. All berries are a good source of antioxidants, in particular polyphenols, however, blueberries have the highest antioxidant levels. They are also a source of omega-3 and pack a great punch of sweet flavour, which dogs just love.

**BROCCOLI:** dark green vegetables are superfoods for dogs as well as humans. Broccoli provides a hearty dose of fibre, needed for healthy digestion, as well as many vitamins and minerals, such as iron.

**BUTTERNUT SQUASH:** is rich in beta-carotene, which is used by dogs to make vitamin A. As it's important for maintaining good vision, a regular dose of vitamin A is especially beneficial for older dogs. Butternut is also packed with immune-boosting alpha-carotene, lutein and zeaxanthin (all carotenoids). It's rich in lots of other complex sounding things too: pantothenic acid, folate, niacin and more. Trust me, they're all beneficial. Butternut squash is a wonderful thing!

**CABBAGE:** another healthy green vegetable, with an antioxidant and iron boost for your pup. But be careful not to feed them too much or your nose may regret it; some dogs get a little gassy with too much cabbage or dark greens.

**CARROTS:** are rich in beta-carotene which is turned into vitamin A in the body, and is important for vision and immunity. It's also a powerful antioxidant, providing protection from cell damage and supporting a healthy immune system. Studies show that absorption rates for beta-carotene are increased by cooking.

**CRANBERRIES:** superfood cranberries pack a serious antioxidant punch and a powerful kick of vitamin C. Apart from all that, dogs relish their sweet flavoursome addition to baked recipes.

**GREEN BEANS:** these are one of my top treat recommendations for dogs needing to lose some weight. They are slightly sweet with a delectable crunch dogs enjoy, and are high in beneficial fibre. Feed them on their own raw, cooked into a recipe, or stuffed in a puzzle feeder with some lean meat.

**KALE:** a great dark leafy green, high in fibre, vitamins A, C and E, iron and other goodies. Like cabbage, go easy at first if your dog's not used to it, as some dogs get gassy.

**MINT:** contains beneficial compounds with deodorising and antibacterial properties. So it's great for dental and oral health, and can mask doggy breath with its delicious scent.

**PARSLEY:** contains high levels of chlorophyll and other beneficial compounds which are thought to have antibacterial and deodorising properties.

**PARSNIP:** much like carrots and other root vegetables, parsnips are a great source of soluble and insoluble fibre, which may help dogs with digestive issues and encourage healthy gut flora.

**PEAS:** whole peas contain beneficial antioxidants, as well as fibre and a wide range of nutrients such as vitamins C, K and B1, manganese and folate.

**TOP TIP!**

Start as young as possible with healthy treats, to help with lifetime weight control. Most dogs love the sweet crunch of carrots or green beans just as much as more calorific treats.

**PUY LENTILS:** a good source of plant-based protein and amino acids to complement animal sources. They also provide a great feeling of fullness for hungry dogs and so are useful for dogs on a weight-loss diet.

**RASPBERRIES:** berries are a good source of vitamin C, dietary fibre, potassium and a powerful source of antioxidants, in particular polyphenols. And it's in our dogs' natures to graze on delicious berries when they find them in season.

**RED PEPPER:** colourful peppers are a great source of beta-carotene, vitamins C and E, and other antioxidants. Be careful to introduce peppers in small quantities at first to get your dog's digestive system used to them, as some dogs can experience an upset stomach if fed too much, too soon.

**SAGE:** like mint and parsley, sage has potent antioxidant action and may have some beneficial antibacterial effects too.

**SPINACH:** is a good source of vitamins, minerals and chlorophyll. And it has a great variety of antioxidants, from beta carotene, vitamin C and alpha-lipoic acid to lutein and zeaxanthin.

**STRAWBERRIES:** contain good levels of vitamin C and plant polyphenols. They are high in sugar, so should be used sparingly, but they do contain some fibre, which can reduce blood sugar spikes.

**SWEDE:** contains soluble and insoluble fibre. Both types together can help restore digestive health as part of a balanced diet by encouraging healthy gut flora. Great if your pup has sensitive digestion.

**SWEET POTATOES:** are scrumptious to dogs. They are nutritionally quite different from normal potatoes; they contain much more fibre, are a fantastic source of vitamin A, and are rich in vitamins C and B6 as well as several minerals. Sweet potatoes are also rich in bioflavonoids – compounds which have been shown to help stabilise blood sugar levels and so can be a useful component of the diet for diabetic dogs.

**THYME:** may provide some benefit for oral or dental health as it has mild antiseptic properties. But including thyme in your dog's treats doesn't mean you should neglect other dental hygiene efforts like brushing, regular vet checks and dental chews.

## TOP TIP!

If your dog has inflamed gums, stained teeth or really bad breath, I'd recommend a vet check rather than relying on fresh breath treats or dental chews exclusively.

# Supplements

By supplements I don't mean artificial pills from the health food shop. I mean real, honest, natural ingredients which, when used in the right quantities, can benefit your dog's overall health.

As a vet, it's important to seek out and back up any dietary claims I make with evidence. So I've only included ingredients that have been proven to have some health benefit to dogs. Where the evidence is a little weaker, or there may be some debate as to how effective certain ingredients are, I'll be sure to say things like 'may be beneficial for' rather than 'proven to'. Rest assured, there's nothing in this book that can cause your dog harm if you follow the recipes I've provided, and take into account their individual allergies or intolerances.

**BLACK PEPPER:** you may notice that throughout this book I include black pepper alongside turmeric. Turmeric is very much in fashion right now for its potential anti-inflammatory effects, specifically for arthritis or joint pain. But studies have shown that the active compound in turmeric, curcumin, is actually activated and becomes more potent with black pepper present too.

**CAROB:** a naturally sweet chocolate alternative, as chocolate is toxic to dogs. It also contains some vitamin A, B2, B3, B6 and D, plus calcium, magnesium, iron, potassium and a small amount of protein.

**CHAMOMILE:** this herb is widely claimed to have calming or anti-anxiety effects in people. The jury is out on whether the same is true for dogs, but it's certainly not harmful to try it as an anti-anxiety aid in fearful dogs.

**CINNAMON:** studies on other animals and humans showed improved memory and brain performance with this spice, so the same may be true in dogs. It's also been shown to be beneficial in regulating blood glucose and insulin levels, and one study suggested some cardiac-supportive effects. Cinnamon isn't suitable for dogs during pregnancy.

**COCONUT OIL (OR COCONUT FLOUR):** a popular, flavoursome ingredient that is sometimes claimed to cure all ills. Coconut oil does provide a beneficial type of fat – medium chain triglycerides (MCTs) – which can support skin health. It has also been linked with reducing seizures in epileptic dogs if used in very specific quantities. But a warning about its use: it is higher in saturated fat than butter, beef fat or lard, so it's extremely high in calories. Use sparingly (if at all, if your dog is already struggling with weight) and approach the hype with a little caution. It's not the magic elixir some internet articles might have you believe.

**GINGER:** contains essential oils, beta-carotene, acetic acid, alpha-linolenic acid, ascorbic acid, camphor, capsaicin and gingerols – good stuff all round! Ginger is well known for its anti-nausea and digestive benefits, but human studies have also revealed the anti-inflammatory effects of ginger, which may also be beneficial for dogs. Both human and animal studies have shown that supplementing ginger can improve cognitive function and memory.

**LINSEED:** also known as flax seed, linseed is a good source of dietary fibre and protein. It's a great source of ALA (alpha-linolenic acid), an omega-3 that supports healthy skin and coat, and also contains the similarly named linoleic acid, an omega-6 fatty acid. For optimal nutrition, omega-3 and -6 need to exist alongside each other in balance.

**OLIVE OIL:** full of essential fatty acids and vitamin E for healthy skin and coat, olive oil can be a useful addition to recipes for dogs with skin conditions.

**PUMPKIN AND PUMPKIN SEEDS:** the orange flesh is a great source of soluble fibre, vitamin C and beta-carotene. The seeds contain glutamate and L-tryptophan, which may help decrease fear and anxiety in dogs by boosting anti-stress chemicals and the production of the happy hormone serotonin in the brain.

**RAPESEED OIL:** is low in saturated fat, but has a high omega-3 fat content, which can help with skin and coat health.

**SUNFLOWER OIL:** is low in saturated fat and rich in the natural antioxidant vitamin E.

**TURMERIC:** contains an active compound called curcumin, which is widely claimed to have potent anti-inflammatory effects, and is said to ease the pain of arthritis and other inflammatory conditions in humans and dogs. The difficulty is that there's a lot of conflicting evidence. Some studies say the amounts required to see any benefit would be huge and impractical to consume, even potentially harmful. Others suggest that there may be mild improvements in dogs' lameness. One interesting finding is that the anti-inflammatory action of curcumin is increased when used in conjunction with black pepper. So my view is this: it's unlikely to do your dog any harm, and it may have some beneficial effects alongside a little black pepper, but if your dog is very lame or stiff you probably should be using it alongside other joint supplements and perhaps even anti-inflammatory medication prescribed by your vet.

**YEAST:** a good source of natural B vitamins, which aid digestion and metabolism, support the nervous system, and keep the skin, hair, eyes, mouth and liver healthy. Yeast is also a good source of protein – it is known as a 'complete protein' since it contains all ten of the essential amino acids needed by dogs. And despite confusion, yeast in food is totally different to the yeast skin infections some dogs suffer from; the two aren't linked.

# Foods to Avoid

It's easy to think that if something is safe for us to eat, it must be safe for our dogs too. But that's not always true – some foods are toxic to dogs, containing substances that are harmful to their health. In extreme cases, eating them can be fatal. Here are eight of the most important foods (or drinks) that you should never feed your dog, as well as nine more that have the potential to make your dog unwell and so are best avoided.

## Foods that are toxic:

**1. ALCOHOL:** alcohol affects dogs more intensely than it affects humans, and can cause damage to multiple organs, like kidneys, liver and stomach. Be particularly careful if sweet alcoholic drinks are around, as sugar can cover up the alcohol flavour that would normally put dogs off.

**2. APPLE PIPS:** while apple is OK to give your dog in small amounts, it's important not to serve the whole fruit. That's because apple pips contain cyanide. Ditch the core, and serve tasty pip-free slices instead.

**3. CAFFEINE:** the stimulant effect of caffeine is bad news for dogs – it can make them anxious, hyperactive, and affect their heart. In serious cases, it can even cause them to collapse or have a seizure. The high caffeine content of coffee puts it among the worst offenders, so always keep your morning brew out of your dog's reach.

**4. BLUE CHEESE:** the fungus that makes blue cheese taste delicious to humans is far from friendly to our pet pals. That's because it releases roquefortine C – a toxin that, in severe cases, can cause tremors and seizures.

**5. CHOCOLATE:** chocolate is well known for being poisonous to dogs as it contains theobromine, a substance similar to caffeine. All chocolate is a no-go, but dark chocolate should be kept especially off-limits, thanks to higher levels of this harmful substance.

**6. GRAPES, RAISINS AND CURRANTS:** while it's not clear exactly what makes these foods toxic for dogs, they've been associated with symptoms as severe as kidney failure – so they're best avoided.

**7. ONIONS, GARLIC AND LEEKS:** all contain thiosulphate, a substance known to cause tummy troubles and a severe form of anaemia. It's not just the whole vegetables you need to keep out of your dog's reach – garlic and onion flavourings can appear in almost any savoury dish, including baby food.

**8. XYLITOL:** look out for this common artificial sweetener that's toxic for dogs. It's often in things you wouldn't expect, like baked goods and peanut butter.

# Foods that are potentially harmful:

**1. AVOCADO:** while avocado flesh can be ok in small quantities, the skin, leaves and stem contain more persin – a chemical that doesn't agree with dogs' digestion and can be harmful. The stone also poses a choking hazard.

**2. BONES:** 'give the dog a bone' is fine for a nursery rhyme, but in real life dogs and bones are a riskier mix. Raw bones can carry nasty bacteria that may upset your dog's stomach. Meanwhile, cooked bones are brittle – pieces can break off and get stuck in your dog's throat or digestive system, or even pierce your dog's intestine walls.

**3. CITRUS FRUITS:** ignore the videos of dogs eating lemons; citrus fruits and dogs aren't a good combination. The citric acid and essential oils found in oranges, lemons, limes and grapefruit are known to upset a dog's digestive system – among other symptoms.

**4. HIGH-FAT, SALTY OR FRIED FOODS:** rich, fatty foods have a nutrient balance that's out of sync with what's healthy for dogs. Salty foods can make your dog thirsty, and need to urinate more. That means crisps and chips are off the menu.

**5. MILK AND OTHER DAIRY PRODUCTS:** most dogs can't digest lactose – a type of sugar found in milk – so dairy products often cause digestive upsets in our canine companions.

**6. MUSHROOMS:** it's best to keep mushrooms out of your dog's diet altogether, so they're not tempted by the potentially poisonous ones you see out and about.

**7. MACADAMIA NUTS:** some nuts may be healthy for humans, but they can leave dogs extremely unwell. Macadamia nuts are particularly problematic, as they can cause vomiting, fever and muscle weakness.

**8. OUT-OF-DATE FOOD:** make sure you bin out of date food somewhere your dog can't get to it, as it's likely to make them unwell. If it's past the point where you'd eat it, don't let your dog eat it either.

**9. SHELLFISH:** dogs can eat fish, so you might expect shellfish to be fine too. But foods like crab, prawns and crayfish can contain pathogens that make your dog extremely unwell. Shellfish can also cause an allergic reaction in dogs, thanks to high levels of an amino acid called histidine.

**SUMMARY:**

– Different ingredients have different health benefits for our dogs.

– Your dog's diet needs to include a healthy balance of protein, fat, carbohydrate, vegetables and supplements.

– There are some foods that you should never feed to your dog.

# Feed Your Dog the Right Amount

Studies have shown that by keeping our dogs in ideal body condition, they can actually live longer.

And their quality of life is better when they are nice and trim: less stiffness, better mobility, keeping that joyous puppy tail wagging for longer.

Most of us overestimate just how much food our dogs need, and underestimate how much we are truly giving them. An appropriately sized portion of quality dry kibble for a dog ten times smaller than us will, of course, look measly to us. But it's rich, concentrated nutrition, and just because they look at us for food doesn't necessarily mean they are actually hungry. It's in a dog's instinct to eat as much as possible – and they have an amazing ability to never lose their appetite! It's up to us to regulate the amount of food we give them.

While no one wants to dwell on negatives, we can't write a book about treating our pets without mentioning the problem of pet obesity. Recent estimates suggest that over 50 per cent of dogs in the UK are overweight or obese. It's difficult to recognise overweight pets as it's so common, we see it everyday. As a vet, it's a frustrating situation; I understand why it happens, but I also see the complications of managing our pets' health when they're on the heavy side. So let's talk for a second about healthy weight management.

Over 50 per cent of dogs in the UK are overweight or obese

When it comes to the crunch, if the amount of food we feed our dog provides more calories than they burn off through activity, they'll end up gaining weight. Exercise is important for physically burning off energy, as well as for mental stimulation, but the real way we can control our dogs' weight is in how much we feed them.

We need to count everything that passes our dogs' lips as food. I know it's tempting to slip them a slice of toast, or an extra few biscuits. Even the habit of 'measuring' by eye how much dry food we're putting in their bowl can mean we're giving them too much. Every treat (including the ones in this book) counts, so make sure you're honest with yourself about how much they are getting day by day, week by week.

As the scales only tell you so much, the Body Condition Score (see pages 42–3) is a great tool for literally getting to grips with whether your dog is overweight, underweight or in ideal shape. Once you've assessed all three areas covered in the BCS technique, you can give your dog a score on the scale from 1–5, to truly determine if they are at a healthy weight for their size. If they're not at an ideal BCS (a score of 3), then you can alter their portions to get them back to a healthy condition.

Like most things, practice makes perfect, so carrying out the test frequently is a good idea. If you're trying to help your dog lose or gain weight, once a month is recommended; if your dog is at an ideal weight, every two months is a good idea, so you notice any changes in time.

If you have completed the BCS and found your dog needs a little help getting back in shape, there are a few things you can do today that will start them in the right direction:

Studies have shown that by keeping our dogs in ideal body condition, they can actually live longer

**1** Keep a food diary for an entire week of everything you're giving them (including treats the rest of the family may be sneaking them!).

**2** Swap out their usual treats for healthier, lower calorie ones. The recipes for Calming Halloween Pumpkin Chews (page 95) and Frozen Chicken & Apple Bites (page 69) are a good place to start.

**3** Always reduce the amount in their main meals if you've given them extra treats, scraps, or titbits that day.

**4** If they're struggling to lose weight, book in with the vet or vet nurse in your local practice to discuss a weight management programme.

If you carry out the assessment and determine that your dog is an ideal BCS, simply maintain healthy habits. This book should help you, alongside the right diet, exercise and portion control.

## SUMMARY:

– Obesity in dogs can lead to various health conditions that may reduce your dog's enjoyment of life.

– Carrying out a BCS assessment can help you to know if your dog is a healthy weight.

– As well as the right diet, it's important to control your dog's portion sizes and treat responsibly.

# Body Condition Score (BCS)

By getting hands-on and assessing three key areas on your dog, you can work out if they are underweight, overweight or in ideal condition. The three areas to examine and feel are:

– ribs
– belly
– waist

Once you've assessed these three areas, you give them a score on a five-point scale, as below.

## RIBS
—

**What to do:**
Run your fingers over your dog's rib cage, on either side of their chest in a head to tail direction.

**What should you feel?**
You should be able to feel the ribs with a slight covering of muscle over them, but they shouldn't be visible, feel like sharp ridges or be poking out. It's important to really feel them with your fingertips rather than just looking, as many dogs' coats will hide the ribs from view.

LOW SCORING: If your dog is under-weight, their ribs will protrude and feel sharp or bumpy as you run your hands along them. If this is the case, it'll mean a lower BCS.

HIGH SCORING: If your dog is overweight the ribs will be difficult to feel as they will be covered in a layer of fat and muscle. The deeper the ribs are to feel under this layer, the more overweight your dog is and the higher the BCS.

## BELLY
—

**What to do:**
Run your hand along your dog's underside, again from head to tail end and also look at the belly from the side.

**What should you feel?**
The belly or undercarriage should start low to the ground where it meets the sternum (or breastbone) at the bottom of the rib cage. Then it should slope higher the further back towards the hips you run your hands on either side.

LOW SCORING: An underweight dog with a lower BCS will have a very pronounced 'tummy tuck' up towards the hips and groin region.

HIGH SCORING: If the belly droops or hangs down near the floor all the way along and doesn't tuck up underneath the hips then your dog may be carrying excess weight and have a higher BCS.

# WAIST
—

**What to do:**
Looking down on your dog's waist and hips from above, you should notice that this area is much narrower than the width of the chest and ribcage.

**What should you feel?**
A slowly tapering abdomen leading from the wider chest to a narrow waist is the sign of an ideal body condition.

LOW SCORING: An underweight dog will have a noticeably narrow waist and the bones of the hips and spine may be easily visible and can be felt protruding under the skin. The more pronounced these bony projections, the more underweight they are and hence the lower their BCS.

HIGH SCORING: In overweight or obese dogs, the waist does not narrow towards the hips. The trunk or abdomen will often be just as wide as the chest, giving them a barrel-shaped appearance. In dogs with a very high BCS, there may even be fat pads at the waist which stick out even further than the width of the chest when viewed from above.

**1**

**Severely underweight**

Very thin with ribs and pelvis prominent

**2**

**Underweight**

Below ideal weight with ribs and waist visible

**3**

**Ideal**

Good condition, some fat cover but ribs easy to feel

**4**

**Overweight**

Above ideal weight. Ribs hard to feel, no obvious waist visible

**5**

**Obese**

Very over-weight with rolls of fat and large abdomen

# A Final Word on Taste

Your dog has to enjoy their food! Many factors affect our dogs' enjoyment of food, and one may surprise you: it's you, and your reaction to their food.

Sometimes dogs will take cues from us when they are about to try a new food – if you're excited about it, they will be too. If they know they can refuse dog food and their worried owner will cook them roast chicken instead, many dogs will hold out for the roast chicken; they are quite clever really!

When you do choose to treat your dog with the foods they love, harness that drool appeal to teach an old dog new tricks. High-reward treats with moreish flavours, such as bacon, work as great motivators in training and obedience games (see pages 54–5). I believe in you, and the power of these treats.

The recipes I've created here are delicious and delightful for dogs, but they don't replace a balanced diet of quality dog food formulated by a qualified animal nutritionist. Use the recipes in this book as an occasional reward and resist caving in to those puppy dog eyes every time they tug at the heartstrings. Choosing the right diet for your dog – supplemented with these goodies, rather than based on them – will result in a longer, happier and healthier life for our dogs. A goal we all can agree on.

If you're excited about it, they will be too

# Spring

# Cleo's Chicken & Apple Balls

Cleo is my daughter's nine-month-old Maltipoo. I've worked with my fair share of fussy babies and toddlers, but she's definitely up there as a picky pooch. So I thought I'd adapt my famous chicken and apple balls for Cleo. This recipe was born out of my attempts to get my fussy son to eat chicken, and incorporating apple worked a treat. So much so, it's become one of my most popular recipes of all time, so why should dogs miss out?

Cooked chicken is a good source of protein for kids and canines, although in revising this recipe for Cleo, I removed the onion. I love to add natural flavour to children's food, but onion is toxic for dogs and can make them very sick.

*– Annabel*

**MAKES: 30 BALLS**
—

**Prep:** 15 minutes
**Cook:** 15 minutes

- 600g skinless chicken thigh fillets, roughly chopped
- 1 small eating apple, peeled and grated
- ½ red pepper, diced
- 1 medium carrot, peeled and grated
- 20g dairy-free Parmesan-style cheese, grated
- 2 tsp chopped fresh sage

Preheat the oven to 200°C (fan)/gas 7 and line a baking tray with non-stick baking paper.

Put the chicken thighs into a food processor and whiz until finely chopped. Squeeze out any excess water from the apple and add to the processor along with all the remaining ingredients. Whiz again until the mixture comes together.

Shape the mixture into 30 small balls, each approximately 4cm in diameter. Place them on the prepared baking sheet. Bake in the preheated oven for 15 minutes, or until cooked through. Remove the tray from the oven and allow the balls to cool a little.

Store in an airtight container in the fridge for up to 5 days, or freeze for up to 3 months.

# Good Boy Beetroot & Cheese Bone Biscuits

This is a great recipe to get even the smallest of hands involved. Making cookie dough is super fun, and the kids will love using bone-shaped cutters.

I tend to batch-cook these biscuits and take a few with me when we go on long walks. Our dogs 'fetch' at lightning speed when they know these are being dangled as a reward.

Beetroot is a great ingredient as it's packed with vitamins and minerals, which are good for your dog's digestion and immune system as well as healthy skin and coat. While it's rare, some dogs can be allergic, so monitor your dog if you decide to feed them beetroot.

*– Annabel*

**MAKES: ABOUT 30 (DEPENDING ON CUTTER SIZE)**
—

**Prep:** 20 minutes
**Cook:** 1 hour

150g cooked beetroot, sliced
275g plain flour, plus extra for dusting
½ tsp baking powder
½ tsp bicarbonate of soda
200g dairy-free margarine
200g dairy-free Cheddar-style
  cheese, grated

+ a bone-shaped cookie cutter

Preheat the oven to 160°C (fan)/gas 4 and line two baking trays with non-stick baking paper.

Put the beetroot into a food processor and whiz until smooth. Add all the remaining ingredients and process until combined.

Dust the work surface with a little flour. Knead the mixture until you have a workable dough. Roll out the dough to 1½cm thick and cut out shapes using the cookie cutter.

Place the dough shapes on the prepared baking trays and bake for 1 hour, or until lightly golden. Leave to cool on a wire rack.

Store the biscuits in an airtight container for up to 5 days, or freeze for up to 3 months.

# Lamb, Pea & Mint Feast

**MAKES: AS MANY SERVINGS YOUR LEFTOVERS WILL STRETCH TO**

—

**Prep:** 10 minutes

mashed potato (kept aside before any salt, butter or gravy is added) – this needs to make up at least 50% of the ingredients

cooked lamb (grilled or roasted), visible fat removed and chopped into small pieces

steamed or boiled peas (or you can substitute green beans or carrots if you have those)

a few sprigs of fresh mint, finely chopped

+ a puzzle feeder dog toy

This recipe can be cooked especially for your dog, or you can use leftovers from your Sunday roast, with a few considerations to make it suitable and safe for dogs (see pages 88–9). My inspiration for this feast is not just to provide your dog with super tasty, nutritious food, but also to give you ideas for occupier treats. Simply popping leftovers into their bowl to be gobbled up in seconds wastes a precious opportunity to stimulate our dogs' minds. Pop it into a puzzle feeder, however, and you can provide all-important mental stimulation, too.

—

Mix the ingredients together thoroughly.

Spoon the mixture into the puzzle feeder until it's tightly packed.

Serve fresh there and then. Alternatively, prepare a few and wrap in cling film before freezing, ready to pull out and use when you need.

## IMPORTANT !

Don't be tempted to use roast potatoes combined with lamb as they're too fatty for dogs and could trigger pancreatitis or digestive upsets.

# Maximising Treat Benefit

The beauty of 'high-reward' treats – with flavour combinations that dogs just can't get enough of – is that they will do anything for them!

It's very easy to feed our dogs one treat after the other passively, and unfortunately this is also a recipe for overfeeding – especially if we don't exercise them enough. Instead, use these delectable doggy treats in creative ways to stimulate and entertain. And while most dogs aren't too fussy about their treats, find the flavours they love the most and you will have them doing the tango for that treat! Experiment with some of the recipes and see what comes up tops.

A tired dog is
a happy dog!

## THE BENEFITS OF TREATING
—

As if the nutritious recipes themselves aren't enough reason to treat your dog, here are some added benefits:

### Quality time together
The greatest reward for your dog is attention from and interaction with you. Spending time teaching them skills – encouraged by a well-earned treat when they master a trick – is one of the best ways to nurture the dog–owner relationship.

### Relief from boredom
Many behavioural problems stem from dogs not being mentally stimulated enough. They are clever animals, and if not entertained, they have been known to seek out their own entertainment in more mischievous ways!

### It's natural and enjoyable
Dogs love working for their food. It's unnatural for animals to have food presented to them in a bowl – in the wild they would spend the majority of their time seeking it out. Creating a barrier to their receiving food – a physical challenge or a problem to be solved – is highly rewarding for them.

### Physical exercise
Encourage your dog to work for their treats, either by focused training sessions, teaching them new commands or by playing games with them. Even hiding treats around the garden for them to hunt out can help to increase exercise levels. My favourite saying is 'A tired dog is a happy dog!'

# PUZZLE FEEDERS

If you are struggling to find enough time for your dog around work or other family commitments, puzzle feeders and other occupiers can be a brilliant distraction. Popping a treat or two into one of these devices whilst you go out to work might just mean you find your furniture spared when you come home at the end of the day! Here are some of our favourites, and their benefits:

## Slow feeding bowls

Not only do these keep your dog occupied, but they have the added benefit of stopping them inhaling their food, and therefore can help relieve some digestive (or indigestive as the case may be!) upsets.

## Wobblers

These stand upright, and dispense treats through a small hole when pushed in the right direction. As they wobble, roll and spin unpredictably, your dog will need to have some patience and cunning to work out the best way to extract the treats.

## Puzzle balls

Great for physical exercise as well as mental stimulation, puzzle balls capitalise on the never-waning excitement dogs have for balls! Hide a few treats inside and your dog will have an added incentive to chase a ball around for hours.

## Snuffle mats

Sprinkle treats into a snuffle mat and your dog will need to sniff their way through folds of fabric to find their hidden treat.

# OCCUPYING IDEAS

With or without a puzzle feeder, there are plenty of ways to keep your dog occupied. Any food can be an occupier treat if you incorporate an element of challenge.

## Put your treats on ice

If you want to add another level of intricacy, freeze the treats to make extraction from a puzzle feeder more difficult. Put small treats (or kibble) into a feeder, fill with water and freeze. Revel in the sight of your hound going to town on a frozen feeder toy meat feast!

## Divide up the dinner

Rather than giving your dog their food in one bowl, divide it into lots of small bowls and hide them all in different places outside – they'll enjoy sniffing out their supper. And you could even try tucking yourself away with one of the bowls for a classic game of hide and seek!

## Try a classic magic trick

Hide your dog's treats under one of three plastic cups. Mix the cups up, with doggy watching, and let them pick the cup containing the reward.

## Create an agility course

Making a DIY obstacle course can be a brilliant way to tire out your dog mentally and physically. Introduce hoops to jump through, blankets to crawl under, poles to slalom around or paddling pools to splash through – use your imagination. The harder you make the course, the tastier the reward for your dog for making it through!

# Carrot & Parsley Minty-Fresh Bones

**MAKES: ABOUT 30 (DEPENDING ON CUTTER SIZE)**

—

**Prep:** 20 minutes
**Cook:** 25 minutes

200g rice flour, plus extra for dusting
25g rolled oats
2 carrots, washed and grated
handful of fresh parsley, finely
  chopped
handful of fresh mint, finely chopped
45g xylitol-free peanut butter

+ a bone-shaped cookie cutter

## IMPORTANT!

Some peanut butters contain the artificial sweetener xylitol, which is toxic to dogs. Make sure you choose a xylitol-free peanut butter.

These treats are not only highly nutritious, but can help with doggy breath and provide dental health benefits too! Parsley and mint have antibacterial and deodorising effects – great for freshening breath. Along with carrots, these plant ingredients are also rich in antioxidants to boost immune function. Dog breath be gone!

—

Preheat the oven to 180°C (fan)/gas 6 and line two baking trays with non-stick baking paper.

Combine the flour and oats in a large bowl, then stir in 150ml water. Add the grated carrots, chopped herbs and peanut butter. Stir thoroughly, until a thick dough is formed.

Sprinkle some flour on a work surface and roll out the dough to 6–8mm thick. Cut out individual treats with the cookie cutter and place them on the prepared baking sheet.

Bake the bones in the preheated oven for 20–25 minutes until golden brown. The cooking time will vary according to the thickness of your treats. Allow to cool on a wire rack before serving.

Store the biscuits in an airtight container for up to a week, or freeze for up to 3 months.

# Cranberry & Linseed Valentine Hearts

**MAKES: 30–35 HEARTS (DEPENDING ON CUTTER SIZE)**

—

**Prep:** 20 minutes
**Cook:** 18 minutes

180g wholemeal flour (or rice flour if intolerant to wheat), plus extra for dusting
50g dried cranberries
3 tbsp linseed
45g rolled oats
2 eggs
1 tbsp rapeseed or sunflower oil
3–4 tbsp ground almonds

+ a heart-shaped cookie cutter

These yummy biscuits are a special and nutritious treat for your dog on Valentine's Day – or any other time you want to pamper your pooch.

Cranberries are a true superfood, bursting with immune-boosting antioxidants and vitamin C. Linseed is a great source of ALA (alpha-linolenic acid), an omega-3 fatty acid, as well as omega-6, both of which support healthy skin and coat. If your dog could talk, he'd say: 'Show me the love!'

—

Preheat the oven to 160ºC (fan)/gas 4 and line two baking trays with non-stick baking paper.

Mix the flour, cranberries, linseed and rolled oats in a bowl.

In another bowl, beat the eggs, then mix in the oil. Add this to the dry ingredients and mix well until an even, sticky dough is formed.

Add the ground almonds, a tablespoon at a time, mixing until the dough is less sticky and easier to handle (you may not need it all).

Sprinkle some flour on a work surface and roll out the dough to 6–8mm thick. Cut out hearts with the cookie cutter and place them on the prepared baking tray.

Bake the hearts in the preheated oven for 16–18 minutes until crisp and golden brown. Allow them to cool on a wire rack before sharing the love with your pup.

Store the biscuits in an airtight container for up to a week, or freeze for up to 3 months.

# Sean's Pup-Friendly Hot Cross Buns

**MAKES: 12**

—

**Prep:** 30 minutes, plus 1½ hours proving
**Cook:** 15 minutes

350g strong white bread flour
    (or rice flour if intolerant to wheat),
    plus extra for dusting
1 tsp ground cinnamon
20g xylitol-free peanut butter
1 tbsp honey, plus optional extra
    to glaze
2 tsp fast action dried yeast
1 egg
150ml lactose-free milk
1 small carrot, washed and grated
80g dried cranberries
olive oil, for greasing
50g plain flour (or rice flour)

Everyone loves a hot cross bun! But they're not suitable for dogs. Human recipes contain raisins, sultanas, citrus zest and nutmeg – all toxic to our canine companions. Slathering them in butter isn't going to do your pup's waistline any favours either. Here's my delicious dog-friendly recipe, which can be shared by *all* of the family at Easter.

—

Sift the bread flour and cinnamon into a bowl. Add the peanut butter and rub together with your fingertips to create a mixture resembling breadcrumbs. Make a well in the centre of your breadcrumb mix and add the honey and yeast.

In a separate bowl, beat the egg and milk together for about 1 minute. Pour the egg and milk mixture into the well, folding and mixing until a dough is formed. (This could also be done in a stand mixer fitted with a dough hook.)

On a lightly-floured surface, knead the dough until smooth and stretchy, then knead in the grated carrot and cranberries. Shape the dough into a ball and place in a bowl. Cover the bowl with a tea towel and leave in a warm place to rise for an hour.

*Continued overleaf* →

Remove the dough from the bowl and knead it on a floured surface, before shaping into a ball again. Return to the bowl and leave to rise for another 30 minutes.

Meanwhile, preheat the oven to 200°C (fan)/ gas 7 and lightly grease a large baking tray.

Divide the dough into 12 equal pieces. Form the pieces into balls, then flatten into bun shapes and place on the prepared baking tray.

Now for the fun bit! Mix the plain flour with 1½–2 tablespoons water, adding it slowly and stirring in until you have a light dough.

Roll small pieces of the dough into ribbons and create traditional crosses on top of the buns. Or try rolling dots and decorating the buns with paw prints!

Once your masterpieces are ready, pop them in the preheated oven and bake for 12–15 minutes until beautifully golden.

An optional extra touch is to lightly paint the surface of the buns with some honey before they cool, to give the buns a glaze.

Store the buns in an airtight container for up to 5 days, or freeze for up to 3 months.

## TOP TIP!

Serve these up to the whole family so your dog doesn't feel left out at Easter, but do take care with portion control; these are a one-off indulgence, and I advise you to reduce the amount you give your dog for dinner that day.

# Summer

# Guilt-Free Breakfast Bakes

**MAKES: 20–25**

—

**Prep:** 10 minutes
**Cook:** 20 minutes

10 free-range eggs
4 tbsp chopped ham
50g spinach, coarsely chopped
handful of fresh parsley, finely
   chopped
1 tsp ground turmeric
1 tsp ground black pepper

+ 2 x 12-hole muffin tins
+ non-stick cooking spray (optional)

## TOP TIP!

The size of your muffins can be adapted to the size of your dog, and you can scale up the quantities for bigger batches, too. If your dog is lucky enough to get one or two of these for breakfast, consider it a meal replacement that day or adapt their usual portions accordingly.

These little baked-egg and ham marvels are a guilt-free way to indulge your dog in a tasty weekend breakfast when they're begging for a sausage or bacon from your plate. Not only are they generally healthy and wholesome, but turmeric and black pepper can be especially beneficial for ageing dogs or those with stiff joints. Make a batch and freeze individually, and you can just defrost them in the microwave when needed.

—

Preheat the oven to 180°C (fan)/gas 6 and grease the muffin tins with cooking spray. (If you are using silicone muffin moulds, they don't need to be greased.)

Whisk the eggs in a mixing bowl, then add the remaining ingredients and stir together well.

Pour the batter into the prepared muffin tins. Make sure to only fill them three-quarters full, as the eggs will expand during cooking.

Bake in the preheated oven for 20 minutes until golden and risen, then allow them to cool in the tins.

Depending on your dog's size, serve 1–2 to small dogs as a meal replacement; large and giant breeds might welcome a meal of 5–6 at a time.

Store the bakes in an airtight container in the fridge for up to 5 days, or freeze for up to 3 months.

# Frozen Chicken & Apple Bites

**MAKES: ABOUT 40 (DEPENDING ON ICE-CUBE TRAY SIZE)**

—

**Prep:** 10 minutes, plus 4–6 hours freezing

½ low-salt chicken stock cube
450ml boiling water
2 apples, cored and diced
cooked chicken breast, diced
 (optional)

+ paw- or bone-shaped ice-cube trays
 (but any ice-cube trays will do)

When the kids are tucking into cooling ice lollies during summer, know that you can keep all the 'children' happy – including the furry ones! These refreshing summer treats are incredibly tasty for your dog, and the texture of the apple and chicken bits in the ice cube is really satisfying, too. For even more summer fun, the kids will love helping you make them in cute doggy-themed ice-cube trays.

—

Add the stock cube half to the boiling water and stir until dissolved, then allow the stock to cool.

Divide the apple and chicken pieces between the holes in the ice-cube tray. Pour the cooled stock into the ice-cube trays, filling them almost to the brim.

Freeze and serve on warm summer days, a few at a time. Keep them in the freezer for up to 3 months.

**TOP TIP!**

You don't want these too salty – using just half a stock cube provides a hint of chicken flavour that your dog will love.

# Bow Wow Burgers

Nothing says 'summer' more than the smell of yummy burgers cooking on the barbecue. But did you know that you can treat your four-legged friend to a burger of their own? My Bow Wow Burgers are one of a kind … just like your dog.

These are super healthy, yet unbelievably moreish. My summer gatherings with friends wouldn't be complete without these burgers sizzling away on the 'bark-be-cue'!

You'll see that I've opted for a dairy-free Parmesan cheese. Most dogs are lactose intolerant, and although the odd cheese treat doesn't seem to do any harm for some, there are good alternatives out there. Too much cheese can also cause canine constipation or diarrhoea in the short term.

I've also chosen wholegrain bread as it contains no ingredients that could cause problems with your dog's health – although, be aware that a small number of dogs are intolerant to wheat (see page 29).

*– Annabel*

**MAKES: 10**
—

**Prep:** 20 minutes
**Cook:** 15 minutes

80g sliced wholegrain bread
250g minced beef
100g carrot, grated
30g dairy-free Parmesan-style
   cheese, grated
2 tsp chopped fresh thyme
sunflower oil, for brushing

Preheat the oven to 200°C (fan)/gas 7, or get the barbecue fired-up. If oven baking, line a baking tray with non-stick baking paper.

Put the bread into a food processor and whiz to crumbs. Add the remaining ingredients, except the oil, and whiz until everything is well combined.

Shape the mixture into 10 burgers, each around 6cm in diameter. Place on the prepared baking tray and brush the burgers with the oil. If you are cooking on the barbecue, simply brush the burgers with oil and put them straight onto the grill over the heat.

Bake or barbecue for 15 minutes until golden and cooked through. Let them cool and serve to your queue of canine guests!

Store any leftover burgers in an airtight container in the fridge for up to 5 days, or freeze for up to 3 months.

# Summer Berry Biscuits

**MAKES: 20–30 (DEPENDING ON CUTTER SIZE)**

—

**Prep:** 25 minutes
**Cook:** 18 minutes

400g oats (plus a little extra to roll the treats in)
1 apple, cored and grated
5 strawberries, hulled and halved
1 egg
10 raspberries
20 blueberries

+ dog- and star-shaped cookie cutters

These delicious biscuits are a great everyday treat for your dog (I find them pretty delicious too!). With a healthy antioxidant base from the colourful berries, they're good for the immune system and general health. They are also suitable for dogs who are allergic or intolerant to wheat and gluten.

—

Preheat the oven to 200°C (fan)/gas 7 and line two baking trays with non-stick baking paper.

Put the oats in a food processor and process to a fine powder. Transfer to a bowl.

Put the apple, strawberries, egg and berries into the food processor and blend to a smooth mixture. Add the oat powder back in and blitz again briefly to form a thick, sticky mixture. Leave to stand for 10 minutes.

Lightly dust the work surface with a few more oats (whole this time) and roll the dough out to approximately 12mm thick. Using a cookie cutter of your choice, cut out your biscuits and place them on the lined baking trays.

Bake in the preheated oven for 15–18 minutes or until golden brown (larger biscuits may take slightly longer). Allow to cool on a wire rack before serving.

Store the biscuits in an airtight container for up to a week, or freeze for up to 3 months.

# Bono's Peanut Butter & Banana Ice Cream

Bono is my right-hand man at my recipe photoshoots. He's pretty particular over the food styling, although I'm sure he's more concerned as to where the food is going after it's been photographed!

I recently made an amazing banana ice cream, and whilst we were looking at the finished shots, he managed to lap-up the entire bowl (and looked rather pleased with himself for doing so!). How could I not re-name this recipe after him?

This recipe is great both for dogs who can tolerate dairy and those who are lactose intolerant. I make mine with Greek yoghurt, as I know that my brood can cope with dairy. However, this recipe tastes just as good with a quality dairy-free yoghurt.

Bananas are high in vitamins as well as fibre, which can help if your dog is having gastrointestinal problems. They also contain magnesium, which promotes bone growth and helps the body produce protein and absorb vitamins. However, like with any food item, you should only feed your dog bananas in moderation as they do contain natural sugar.

*– Annabel*

**MAKES: 8 PORTIONS**
—

**Prep:** 10 minutes, plus at least 6 hours freezing

- 4 ripe bananas, sliced
- 4 heaped tbsp smooth xylitol-free peanut butter
- 8 heaped tbsp Greek yoghurt or a dairy-free alternative

Line a baking tray with non-stick baking paper.

Spread the banana slices over the tray and put in the freezer for 3 hours, or until frozen.

Put the frozen bananas into a food processor and add the peanut butter and yoghurt. Blend until smooth and creamy in texture, then spoon into a small container.

Freeze for 3 hours or overnight and your canine cooler is ready to serve. As a treat, add a spoonful or scoop to your dog's bowl (keeping the portion size appropriate to your dog's size).

Keep in the freezer for up to 3 months.

# Autumn

# Sean's Savoury Superfood Muffins

**MAKES: 20–25 MUFFINS**

—

**Prep:** 20 minutes
**Cook:** 55 minutes

| 600g butternut squash, peeled, deseeded and cubed
| 500g salmon fillets
| 120g rolled oats
| 150g rice flour, plus extra if needed
| 1 tbsp ground cinnamon
| 1 tbsp ground ginger
| 135g blueberries
| 1 tbsp ground turmeric (optional)
| 1 tsp ground black pepper (optional)
| 1 tbsp rapeseed oil
| 150ml lactose-free milk
| 1 egg

These muffins are just fantastic for older dogs with stiff joints or arthritis as they are packed with functional ingredients – the salmon is rich in omega-3, while the antioxidants in the berries provide anti-inflammatory action. For an extra supportive boost if your dog is particularly stiff, try adding a little turmeric and black pepper.

The muffins are great to make in batches as they freeze really well.

—

Preheat the oven to 190°C (fan)/gas 6 and line a baking tray with non-stick baking paper.

Place the squash cubes on the prepared baking tray and roast for 20 minutes. Add the salmon fillets to the tray with the squash and bake for a further 15 minutes, then leave to cool. Leave the oven on and re-line the baking tray with clean baking paper.

Meanwhile, in a mixing bowl, combine the oats, flour, cinnamon, ginger, blueberries, and turmeric and black pepper, if using.

Put the cooled salmon and squash in a food processor, add the oil, milk and egg, and blend to a smooth consistency. (If you don't have a food processor, you can finely mash all of the ingredients together with a fork.)

Pour the salmon mixture into the dry mix and fold the ingredients together to form a dough. Roll small pieces of the dough in your hands – flouring your hands if too sticky to roll. Choose an appropriate size for your dog.

Place the dough balls onto the freshly lined tray and bake in the still-hot oven for 15–18 minutes until nicely golden. The larger you make your muffins, the longer they will need. Allow to cool on a wire rack before serving to your dog.

Store the balls in an airtight container in the fridge for up to 5 days, or freeze for up to 3 months.

# Hamilton's Salmon & Puy Lentil Croquettes

Hamilton, my ten-year-old Samoyed, has a problem with the joints in one of his front legs, which means he's also a little overweight as he can't run anymore. His top speed is a stately slow pace ... unless he catches sight of a squirrel!

I always recommend salmon for babies and children as it's packed with those all-important omega-3 fatty acids for brain development. But a good dose of omega-3 also helps control inflammation in the body, which can weaken and disrupt the immune system. And this applies to dogs, too. Salmon is also a great protein source and your dog's personal hairdresser, keeping their coat looking sleek, shiny and healthy.

The Puy lentils in this recipe are a great, low-calorie source of iron and plant-based protein. Their high fibre content helps dogs feel fuller when eating, while keeping blood levels from spiking too sharply after a meal.

– *Annabel*

**MAKES: 12 CROQUETTES**
—

**Prep:** 20 minutes
**Cook:** 20 minutes

250g salmon fillet
75g swede, grated
75g carrot, grated
100g cooked Puy lentils
plain flour, for coating
sunflower oil, for brushing

Preheat the oven to 180°C (fan)/gas 6 and line a baking tray with non-stick baking paper.

Put the salmon, swede, carrot and lentils in a food processor and whiz until finely chopped.

Shape the mixture into 12 sausages and roll each sausage in flour to coat. Arrange the croquettes on the prepared baking tray and lightly brush with oil.

Bake in the preheated oven for 20 minutes, or until lightly golden and cooked through. Allow to cool before plating up for pooch.

Store the croquettes in an airtight container in the fridge for up to 5 days, or freeze for up to 3 months.

# Orchard Fruit Flapjacks

**MAKES: 25 FLAPJACKS**

—

**Prep:** 15 minutes
**Cook:** 20 minutes

200g rolled oats
1 apple, cored and grated
20 ripe blackberries
1½ tbsp honey
3 tbsp sunflower oil
1 tbsp ground cinnamon
1 tbsp ground ginger
1 egg, beaten

+ a 20-cm square baking tin

These are a total favourite of mine; I find them absolutely delicious – as do dogs, more importantly. They are great when out for a hike or a long walk as they are packed with delicious autumn fruit and oats for a slow-release energy hit. They also contain ginger – which can be beneficial for dogs with sensitive digestion – and cinnamon to boost memory and brain function.

—

Preheat the oven to 180°C (fan)/gas 6 and line the baking tin with non-stick baking paper.

Place all of the ingredients in a saucepan and stir over a low heat for 3 minutes to melt the honey and combine everything well.

Tip the mixture into the prepared baking tray. Smooth roughly level, then press the oats down firmly with the back of the spoon or a spatula.

Bake the flapjacks in the preheated oven for 20 minutes, or until a light golden brown. Leave to cool, then remove from the tin and cut into bite-sized chunks.

Serve sparingly as a high-reward treat.

Store the flapjacks in an airtight container for up to a week, but if you taste one for yourself, chances are they won't last that long.

# Feeding Dogs Human Food

If you choose to feed your dog the family meal – they are a member of the family, after all – there are a few simple things to remember.

Many people feed their dogs human food and leftovers. My view is it's OK if you make it an occasional treat and take some simple steps to ensure it's safe. It also goes without saying that it should be instead of, rather than in addition to, their daily food allowance so that they don't gain weight. And there are some benefits to chowing down together:

- It introduces greater variety into their diet, and fresh homemade food can be good for dogs too
- It can help use up leftovers
- Human food is an extra special treat if your dog deserves a reward, and they love the sweet flavour of fresh veggies
- Human food can be great for adding to puzzle feeders, as dogs will really work for it

But there are a few precautions to take if you want to extend your dinner to doggy.

## Ensure the food is safe

This is the most important rule when sharing food. Common flavourings such as garlic and onions are toxic to dogs, and we might not even realise they are hidden in foods, such as gravy or stuffing mixes. Check every ingredient in the foods you are giving them against my list of foods to avoid (pages 36–7). And never allow your dog to scavenge cooked chicken bones, as they are brittle and can splinter in the mouth or, worse, perforate the intestines if swallowed.

## Ensure the food is healthy

While there's a bit less cause for alarm here, feeding our dogs food that's high in fat and salt is not good for them. Fatty foods such as chicken skin and meat juices can upset a dog's digestion or even lead to pancreatitis – a serious and quite painful condition

## Don't do it every day

Remember it's a treat! While dogs can benefit from healthy foods like lean meat and veg in the same way that humans can, their basic nutritional needs are different to ours. Dog food is formulated to meet those needs, so substituting it for human food too often may mean they are not getting what they need.

## Keep an eye on quantity

We all sneak our dog titbits from the table, but it does make it difficult to keep track of how much they have had. If you're going to share, it's better to put a measured portion in a bowl. And by feeding them food from the table, you may be encouraging cheeky begging habits!

# Wheat-Free Bacon & Apple Crunchies

**MAKES: 30–35 CRUNCHIES**

—

**Prep:** 15 minutes
**Cook:** 25 minutes

3 slices of back bacon
200g rice flour
90g rolled oats
1 tbsp ground cinnamon
4 apples, cored
2 eggs
3 tbsp honey

These are a scrummy, high-value training treat; as no dog can resist the taste of bacon and apple, I bet these will help your dog learn a new trick!

Bacon isn't great for dogs as it's very high in fat, but these treats really stretch out the delicious taste of a modest amount. As dogs will munch on as much bacon as you care to give them, you can really harness its appeal without the high-fat hit. Use these as a great way to bond with your hound and encourage some healthy brain training, while sharing the joy of treating.

This recipe is also gluten-free and so is suitable for dogs with allergies or intolerances to wheat.

—

Preheat the oven to 180°C (fan)/gas 6 and line a baking tray with non-stick baking paper.

Trim any visible fat off the bacon slices and grill them until quite crispy. Allow to cool before chopping up into tiny pieces.

Mix the flour, oats and cinnamon in a mixing bowl and make a well in the centre.

Blend two of the cored apples in a food processor to make apple sauce. Grate the other two apples finely and add to the apple sauce.

Mix the eggs, honey and bacon bits into the apple mixture, then pour this wet mixture into the well in your dry mix. Fold together until you get a solid, sticky batter.

Place teaspoon-sized lumps of the mixture onto your prepared baking tray. Bake in the preheated oven for 20–25 minutes until they are nice and crunchy.

Store the crunchies in an airtight container in the fridge for up to 5 days, or freeze for up to 4 months.

# Carrot & Chickpea Pup Pancakes

Pancakes piled high for the whole family to tuck into ... now that's the way to do breakfast at the weekend! I can always guarantee my grown-up children will return home when they know pancakes are on the menu. But they'll always find my dogs first in the queue.

Why not get your family flipping these super-healthy pancakes? Carrots are packed with vitamin A, which helps support doggie immune systems, as well as promote healthy skin and coat and good eyesight. I've also included chickpeas, which are power packed with vitamins, protein, fibre, iron, and more.

– *Annabel*

**MAKES: 16 PANCAKES**
—

**Prep:** 10 minutes
**Cook:** 15 minutes

- 100g cooked chickpeas (drained, tinned chickpeas are fine)
- ½ small carrot (about 50g), grated
- 2 eggs
- 100g self-raising flour
- 150ml oat milk
- 2 tbsp sunflower oil

Put the chickpeas in a food processor and whiz for a few seconds. Add all the remaining ingredients except the oil, and whiz again until blended.

Heat a little of the oil in a large non-stick frying pan. Spoon a heaped tablespoon of batter per pancake into the pan, leaving a little space in between. Fry the pancakes for 2–3 minutes on each side until lightly golden.

Plate up and allow to cool a little, and you'll have your dog barking for brekkie.

Store the pancakes in an airtight container in the fridge for up to 2 days, or freeze, separated by sheets of greaseproof paper, for up to 3 months.

# Calming Halloween Pumpkin Chews

**MAKES: 20–30 CHEWS**

—

**Prep:** 20 minutes
**Cook:** 3–4 hours

2 large sweet potatoes
2 tbsp pumpkin seeds
½ tsp ground turmeric
contents of 1 chamomile tea bag
1 tbsp coconut oil, melted

+ Halloween-themed cookie cutters
(optional)

Halloween can be a scary time for nervous pups, with fireworks and loud bangs at night. These chewy treats not only occupy them with something to get their teeth stuck into, but have calming effects from their ingredients too. Chamomile can be a good herbal aid for anxious dogs. Pumpkin seeds contain L-tryptophan and glutamate, important for the brain to produce the happy hormone serotonin as well as other anti-stress chemicals.

—

Preheat the oven to 100°C (fan)/gas ½ and line 2 baking trays with non-stick baking paper.

Scrub your sweet potatoes but leave the skin on. Slice the sweet potatoes into 8mm thick discs. Cut scary Halloween faces into them using Halloween cookie cutters if you have them, or get arty and (carefully) cut your own face designs. Place them onto the prepared baking trays, making sure they aren't touching each other.

Using a food processor or mortar and pestle, grind the pumpkin seeds into a fine powder.

In a small bowl mix the pumpkin seed powder with the turmeric, chamomile tea and coconut oil. Brush this oil over the top of each sweet potato slice.

Bake in the preheated oven for 3–4 hours until nice and chewy; cook them slightly longer for a crispier treat. For best results, allow them to cool in the oven for a few hours after turning it off.

Store the chews in an airtight container for up to a week.

# Winter

*From Annabel's kitchen:*

—

# Sabre's Beef Stew with Peas

Sabre is a typical golden retriever; he's adventurous in every way, especially when it comes to food. If he were a human, he'd be every parent's dream as he makes light work of veggies and clears his bowl without exception. As an extra special treat, he also loves bacon, although this should only be given in very small amounts on rare occasions, as it is quite fatty.

This recipe is his paws-down favourite. He loves beef, and I've included fresh herbs as they are powerful antioxidants and rich in vitamins. Sage is particularly beneficial as it helps to ease gas or bloating and aids doggy digestion – perfect for Sabre who is our resident 'scoffer' and polishes off his meals in minutes.

A little tip: if your dog demolishes meals in a flash, try using a slow feeder bowl (see page 55), which prevents them from overeating as they have to work harder to get the food. I also sometimes spoon Sabre's food into a muffin baking tin, as moving from cup to cup slows his pace down.

*– Annabel*

**MAKES: 2–3 PORTIONS**

—

**Prep:** 15 minutes
**Cook:** 1¼ hours

1 tsp sunflower oil
100g bacon, diced
400g braising beef, diced
150g carrot, peeled and diced
150ml beef stock
1 tsp chopped fresh thyme
1 tsp chopped sage
100g frozen peas

Preheat the oven to 130°C (fan)/gas 2. Heat the oil in an ovenproof saucepan or casserole dish over a high heat. Add the bacon and beef and fry until sealed. Turn the heat down to medium, add the carrot and fry for a further 2–3 minutes.

Add the beef stock and herbs and cover with a lid. Transfer to the oven and cook for 1 hour until the meat is tender. Remove the pan from the oven, place it back on the hob and add the peas. Heat them for a few minutes until they are cooked through.

Depending on your dog's preference for texture, you can mash the stew a little. Allow to cool down slightly, then serve.

Store in an airtight container in the fridge for up to 4 days, or freeze for up to 3 months.

# Apple, Cranberry & Peanut Butter Oat Cookies

Reward your dog for being your BDF (Best Dog Forever) with these wholesome cookies. Cranberries are high in anti-oxidants and apples are a good source of fibre as well as vitamins A and C. I've also added cinnamon, which acts as an anti-inflammatory, making it a natural muscle relaxant and pain reliever.

Since my dogs have a serious penchant for peanut butter, this recipe receives the paws-up every time.

– Annabel

**MAKES: ABOUT 30 COOKIES (DEPENDING ON CUTTER SIZE)**
—

**Prep:** 20 minutes
**Cook:** 35 minutes

165g coconut flour, plus extra
   for dusting
40g porridge oats
25g desiccated coconut
40g dried cranberries, chopped
40g dried apple, chopped into
   small pieces
1 tbsp ground cinnamon
4 heaped tbsp xylitol-free peanut
   butter
3 eggs, beaten

+ bone- or paw-shaped cookie cutters

Preheat the oven to 140°C (fan)/gas 3 and line two baking trays with non-stick baking paper.

Put the flour, oats, coconut, cranberries, apple and cinnamon into a food processor and whiz until finely chopped. Add the peanut butter, beaten eggs and 6 tablespoons water and whiz again until the mixture comes together into a dough.

Dust the work surface with a little coconut flour. Lightly knead the dough until workable, then roll out to 1½cm thick.

Cut out shapes using doggy cookie cutters to make bones or paws, and lay them on the prepared baking trays.

Bake in the preheated oven for 30–35 minutes, or until lightly browned. Transfer to a wire rack to cool before treating your tail-wagging sidekick.

Store the cookies in an airtight container for up to 3 days, or freeze for up to 3 months.

# Bubble & Squeak Dog Cakes

**MAKES: AS MANY AS YOUR LEFTOVERS WILL STRETCH TO**

—

**Prep:** 10 minutes
**Cook:** 8 minutes per panful

leftover potatoes (mashed, boiled or roasted)
leftover vegetables, such as carrots, parsnip, cabbage
leftover meat, such as turkey and/or ham (optional)
1 egg
a little flour
olive oil, for shallow frying

This is a great, easy way to use up healthy leftovers for an occasional meal of human food for your dog, to replace their main meal of the day. You can use most veg leftovers, but no onions or garlic, which are toxic to dogs (see page 36). Make sure to only use a tiny amount of oil to cook these and make them an appropriate size for your dog. Add in some blueberries if you have them, for an antioxidant boost. Dogs generally love the combination of sweet and savoury, and their ancestors and cousins would naturally have grazed on berries in season.

—

Mash your potatoes (if not already mashed) in a mixing bowl. Add the leftover vegetables and meat, if using, along with the egg, and mash again to combine. Stir in enough flour to give you a mixture firm enough to shape into balls.

Roll the mixture into appropriate-sized balls, then flatten each ball into a burger shape.

Heat a tiny amount of olive oil in a frying pan over a low heat. Once hot, shallow fry the cakes, a few at a time, for 3–4 minutes on each side until golden all over.

Allow to cool before serving.

Store the cakes in an airtight container in the fridge for up to 5 days, or freeze for up to 6 months.

# Healthy 'Yule Dog' Meatloaf

**MAKES: 2 LOAVES**

—

**Prep:** 15 minutes
**Cook:** 1 hour

- 250g of either liver, beef heart or kidney, chopped into small chunks
- 500g turkey mince
- 250g oatmeal
- 50g carrot, diced
- 50g green beans, chopped
- 50g kale, roughly chopped

+ 2 x 450g (1lb) loaf tins

**TOP TIP!**

If you'd prefer not to use offal, replace the liver, heart or kidney with 250g more turkey mince, or even lean beef mince.

At Christmas time, we all give in to the temptation to graze on rich, calorific food around the home. Sweet delights, pigs in blankets, meat sandwiches, cheese: it sets us humans up for weight gain, for sure. But we can easily remove the temptation to indulge our dogs in an unhealthy way. With this recipe, you'll have a healthy, delicious, dog-safe treat to hand. Just a chunk of this meatloaf here and there over the festive period won't do any harm, as long as you subtract a little portion of your dog's regular food in its place.

—

Preheat the oven to 180°C (fan)/gas 6 and line and grease the bottom of your two loaf tins.

Combine all the ingredients in a large bowl and mix well. Divide the mixture evenly between the loaf pans and smooth level.

Bake the loaves in the preheated oven for 1 hour, or until the top is brown and a crust has formed. Pour off any grease before leaving to cool. Once cool, remove from the tins and cut into slices or chunks to serve.

Store the meatloaf in an airtight container in the fridge for up to 5 days. Any excess that won't be used can be frozen. For individual portions, spread bite-sized chunks out on a tray and freeze, then transfer to a container or bag once frozen. They will keep in the freezer for up to 6 months.

# Turkey, Broccoli & Cranberry Bites

**MAKES: 20–30 BITES (DEPENDING ON CUTTER SIZE)**

—

**Prep:** 15 minutes
**Cook:** 25 minutes

5 florets raw broccoli
125g lean turkey mince
120ml low-salt chicken stock
   (or water)
100g dried cranberries
1 tbsp olive oil
1 egg
400g wholemeal flour,
   plus extra for dusting
1 tbsp baking powder

+ a round cookie cutter

It's not just humans that love the turkey–cranberry combo, so delight your doggo with these delectable bites!

Turkey is a great source of lean protein and the amino acid tryptophan, which dogs convert into their happy hormone, serotonin. Christmas can be a stressful time for anxious dogs with lots of visitors, strange sights and smells, and potentially fireworks, so feeding them more turkey can actually be beneficial. If you have leftover cooked turkey, you could use this in place of the turkey mince. Just chop it finely and use as in the recipe.

—

Preheat the oven to 180ºC (fan)/gas 6 and line two baking trays with non-stick baking paper.

Put the broccoli into a food processor and process until finely chopped. Add the turkey mince, stock (or water), cranberries, oil and egg to the broccoli and blend to a smooth consistency.

Mix the flour and baking powder together in a large bowl, then make a well in the centre. Add the wet mixture to the well and fold in to create a firm dough.

On a lightly floured surface, roll out the dough to approximately 12mm thick. Using a cookie cutter, cut out your bites and place them on the prepared baking trays.

Bake the bites in the preheated oven for 20–25 minutes, or until golden brown (larger biscuits will take slightly longer). Allow to cool on a wire rack before serving.

Store the bites in an airtight container in the fridge for up to a week, or freeze for up to 6 months.

# Peanut Butter, Carob & Ginger Tray Bake

**MAKES: 20 SQUARES**

—

**Prep:** 15 minutes
**Cook:** 15 minutes

1 over-ripe banana, peeled
100g xylitol-free peanut butter
1 tsp melted coconut oil (optional)
240g wholemeal flour
½ tsp ground ginger
30g carob powder
1 egg, beaten

+ a deep 20-cm square baking tin

## IMPORTANT!

If your kids are making this recipe, make sure they don't get carob powder mixed up with cocoa powder, which can be very harmful to dogs.

Does your dog give you major guilt face when you're tucking into chocolate? Well, don't give in to those puppy dog eyes because chocolate is toxic for dogs. But that doesn't mean you have to deny them a sweet treat occasionally. Carob is a dog-safe alternative to chocolate you'll find in the baking section of most supermarkets and, combined with peanut butter, it's hard for dogs to resist.

—

Preheat the oven to 200°C (fan)/gas 7 and line the baking tin with non-stick baking paper.

Put the banana in a mixing bowl and mash well. Stir in the peanut butter until you have a smooth, soft, creamy texture. If it doesn't soften and blend well (this may depend on the peanut butter brand), add the coconut oil or a drop of boiling water to help it along.

Add the flour, ginger and carob and stir in, then add the egg and stir everything together well. Transfer the mixture to the prepared baking tray and smooth level.

Bake in the preheated oven for 15 minutes, or until it starts to darken on top. Allow to cool in the tin, then turn out and cut into bite-sized chunks with a pizza roller or knife.

Store the bakes in an airtight container for up to a week.

# Scrummy Sweet Potato & Carrot Birthday Cake

They say you can never spoil a baby – and the same goes for your dog! Birthdays are the perfect opportunity to shower them with infinite amounts of love.

Now that requires a birthday cake of doggy dreams – although you may just need to blow out the candles for them. And I can't promise this won't turn into a cake smash with your doggy delving straight in head first – now that would make for a great Instagram pic!

Packed with my own dog's favourite veggies, this dairy-free mutt masterpiece is the icing on the canine cake when it comes to celebrating their birthday. Now all that's left to do is party with pooch!

*– Annabel*

**MAKES: 1 BIRTHDAY CAKE / SERVES 4**

—

**Prep:** 30 minutes
**Cook:** 45 minutes

1 large sweet potato
150g self-raising flour
1 tsp baking powder
1 medium carrot (about 125g), peeled and grated
2 tbsp honey
3 tbsp melted coconut oil
1 large egg, beaten

**FOR THE TOP:**
1 medium sweet potato
200g dairy-free yoghurt
dog biscuits or other decorations, to garnish

+ an 18-cm round cake tin

*Continued overleaf →*

Preheat the oven to 140°C (fan)/gas 3 and line the cake tin with non-stick baking paper.

Put both sweet potatoes (for the main cake and the icing) into the microwave. Cook at full power for 10 minutes until both are soft. Leave to cool.

Scoop out the flesh of the large sweet potato into a mixing bowl and mash until smooth. Add the flour, baking powder, carrot, honey, coconut oil and egg to the potato and mix until smooth. Spoon the batter into the prepared cake tin and smooth the top.

Pop in the preheated oven and bake for 35 minutes, or until firm in the centre and lightly golden. Leave to cool on a wire rack, then transfer to a plate.

To make the icing, scoop out the flesh of the medium sweet potato into a mixing bowl. Mash it, then add the yoghurt and mix until smooth. Spread the icing evenly over the top of the cake and get creative with decorations. I love to use little dog bones.

Store the cake in an airtight container in the fridge for up to 2 days, but only add the icing just before serving or the cake will go soggy.

**STREETVET**

The proceeds of this book will go to StreetVet, a multi-award-winning charity delivering free care to the homeless and their dogs on the streets throughout the UK.

This is a book for all those dogs lucky enough to have owners prepared to cook delicious treats for them, but we would like the book to also benefit those dogs and owners who aren't lucky enough to have a permanent roof over their heads. And having worked closely with StreetVet for several years we know that the difference they make to the lives of homeless pets and their owners is incredible.

For more information please visit:
www.streetvet.co.uk
Registered charity number: 1181527.

# Index

# Acknowledgements

I'd like to thank tails.com for giving me the opportunity to write this book, and share my passion for helping people make the best choices they can for their pets. To Fiona Wallin for being a brilliant manager and friend (and plenty of giggles along the way); Heidi Cullip for being an all-round superstar, keeping me on track and organised; and Miranda Cresswell for her thoughtful insights on what the reader would really want to hear.

To Galen O'Hanlon and Julia Laguarda for their creative brilliance and ongoing help and support. To Gemma Hosking and all the office dogs and their owners for bringing their energy and fun to the shoots. And thanks to the rest of my tails.com colleagues for being so supportive and rallying around to help whenever needed and make this book a reality.

Big thanks to my mum and dad for nurturing an all-consuming passion in their young son for animals and nature, and for going to great lengths – and making not insignificant sacrifices – to allow me to pursue my dream of becoming a vet.

To Annabel and Sarah for being such lovely partners in writing this book, and inviting us into Annabel's home with such a warm welcome. It's a privilege to collaborate with such a well-respected authority on family nutrition.

Finally to Barry, Dave, Graham and Brian for their help and useful tips on being laser focused on the eve of starting to write this book.

I want to dedicate this book to the lovely Tina, who helped me enormously in my veterinary career and who will be sorely missed.

– *Sean*

First published in 2019 by tails.com

https://tails.com

HB 978-1-91-289261-7
eBook 978-1-91-289262-4

Recipes developed and written by Sean McCormack and Annabel Karmel
Photography by Stuart Ovenden
Food styling by Kat Mead
Props styling by Amy Kinnear
Cover design by Julia Laguarda
Interior page design and layout by Louise Evans
Edited by Rebecca Woods
Project management by whitefox

Select props were generously loaned by:
KONG
Mutts & Hounds
Susie Watson Designs
Sophie Allport

Printed and bound in the UK by Bell & Bain Ltd